Print ISBN: 979-8-9880228-4-8

E-Book ISBN: 979-8-9880228-3-1

Emergency Basics for Everyday People

A Beginner's Guide to Emergency Preparedness, no Tinfoil Hat Needed.

Matthew D. Hunt

Preface

"Emergency Basics for Everyday People" I envisioned this book as a guide for my own college-age children, and those stepping into the realm of independence. I try to break down emergency preparedness essentials in a straight forward way. From fire safety to managing water, electricity, and food, I take a simple, friendly approach. My suggestion? A gradual, budget-friendly strategy that applies to both apartment dwellers and homeowners. Packed with easy-to-follow tips and lists, I encourage you to take small, manageable steps toward everyday safety. Consider this book your perfect companion for those initial steps into the world, something you can keep, refer too, with large, easy to see font, and added space for you to make notes as needed.

Enjoy, and be safe.

Matthew-

Contents

Chapter One

Introduction

Being prepared for an emergency does not make you a Prepper; it just makes you cautious.

Before I start, I will state that these are things that I have learned over the years, things that I have used, and some situations I have been in. **I am sharing this to give you basic ideas and information, but you must decide what is safe for you and your family, what is safe for where you live, and what appropriate actions you should take.** Use common sense; think about what you are doing, and think about fire, water, electrical, food, and safety. Always read the instructions on any item you get and follow those instructions thoroughly.

You will notice that I will repeat myself during this book: Follow instructions, be safe, read labels, think, make sure you test foods, try out and use supplies and appliances before an emergency because there are some people who need to read, see, and hear it many times and that is OK. If you are not one of those readers, great! Ignore and read on.

I will also add that this guide is for everyday people, new homeowners, or young people going out and living on their own. You will not spontaneously grow a beard, have a craving to wear flannel, or build a nuclear fallout shelter out of used tires and cow dung, and this book will not show you how to tame and ride an elk through the forest while overseeing your very own squirrel army. If you are a prepper, you will know most of the information in this book, but you might find some of it helpful or find something you had not thought of (Also, if you

DO know how to tame an elk and create a squirrel army, please reach out. My kids think that would be fun... Actually, so do I.).

Why Prepare?

Look at the last 30 to 40 years: The 1989 earthquake in San Francisco, the L.A. riots, Hurricane Katrina, the fires in California and Oregon, flooding, tornados and hurricanes, water and power supply issues, a pandemic, chemical train derailments, or any of the numerous other emergencies that have happened throughout the world stemming from flooding, fire, earthquakes, tornadoes, hurricanes, and civil unrest. I am sure if you think about it just for a minute, you can remember a time or have lived through a time when you wish you had prepared.

The fact is that we live in an unpredictable world. Emergencies can happen at any time and in any place. It may not always be something as catastrophic as a natural disaster or civil unrest; it could be something as simple as a power outage or losing your job. Whatever the situation may be, being prepared for emergencies can help you and your loved ones stay safe and comfortable during difficult times.

Here are some reasons why it is essential to prepare for emergencies:

1. Safety: The most important reason to prepare for emergencies is for safety. Having emergency supplies such as food, water, first aid kits, and flashlights can help keep you safe during disasters.

2. Self-sufficiency: During an emergency situation, stores may be closed, or supplies may be limited. By having the necessary items on hand, you can become self-sufficient and not rely on outside resources for your basic needs.

3. Peace of mind: Knowing that you are prepared for an emergency allows you to have peace of mind, knowing that you have taken steps to protect yourself and your family.

4. Saves time and money: Being prepared ahead of time can save both time and money in case of an emergency. Instead of rushing to the store to buy supplies at a higher cost during a disaster, having them already on hand will save money in the long run.

5. Helps others: By preparing for emergencies, you can also be in a position to help others.

In many places, like where I live in the Northwest, sometimes it is just simple weather that can get you: With normal winter storms and spring flooding, the power could be out for a day, three days, a week, and in a few places around here it's been out for almost a month at a time. Most of the time, the safest place you can be during an emergency is at home, not running to the store and trying to find essentials along with everyone else.

This guide will not give you everything you need. Only you know what you and your family will need during an emergency. What it will do is provide ideas and basics that you should consider keeping in your home. I will add a few short basic lists to the back of the book to which you can refer and which can be used to supplement your own list of items to keep on hand for an emergency.

Now that you understand the importance of being prepared for emergencies, it's time to start building your emergency supply kit. Remember, this is not a one-size-fits-all situation. You and your family will have specific needs based on your location, health conditions, and personal preferences. It's important to take these into consideration while building your kit.

There are four main staples that you need to survive: water, food, heat, and shelter. This book assumes that you live in an apartment or home. As you read this, I will try to separate what I would suggest for a house and what I would recommend for an apartment. The amount that you are able to set aside will depend on two main things: the room you have in your home and how much money you can spend on your supplies.

Buying supplies is a luxury, so do not go out and spend your whole paycheck on getting all the supplies you need. Take your time. Start with the basics mentioned and go from there, building a little at a time. What supplies I have or will mention in this book are items that I have purchased over the years. I looked for sales and/or great deals on things that I have found a need for or which are a luxury to have in an emergency. So, make yourself a list, and prioritize what you truly need versus what would make life simpler or more enjoyable in the case of an emergency.

Creating Your Emergency Supply List

Before you can start gathering your emergency supplies, you need to have a plan. It's important to make a list of the items you and your family will need during an emergency. This list will serve as a guide to ensure that you don't forget any essentials.

The best way to start this list is by thinking about the things you use on a daily basis. Consider how much of these items your family goes through in two or three weeks. This will give you a reasonable estimate of how much of each item you should have on hand at all times.

Next, think about what types of emergencies are most likely to occur in your area. For example, if you live in an area prone to hurricanes, tornadoes, or snowstorms, you'll want to make sure you have supplies specifically for those types of emergencies. If there are specific health conditions or dietary restrictions in your household, make sure to include any necessary medication or special food items on your list.

Once you have a general idea of what items will be needed for an emergency, it's time to prioritize them. Start with the essentials – water, food, heat, and shelter – and then move on to other necessities such as first aid kits, flashlights, batteries, personal hygiene items, and tools like a can opener or matches.

It's also important not to forget about entertainment and comfort items. While they may not be essential for survival, having things like books, board games, and comfort foods can help keep spirits up during an emergency situation.

Now that you have a list in hand, it's time to start gathering your supplies. Remember to buy only what you can afford at the time and take advantage of sales or discounts when possible.

Tip: Open and try any food or equipment you buy. Confirm the food is something you will eat. Make sure the equipment works, has all its parts, and you know how to use it.

Chapter Two

Overview–Plan

THIS CHAPTER IS JUST AN OVERVIEW.

Don't get overwhelmed! Take it in bits and pieces.

One crucial element to have in any emergency is a well-thought-out plan. This includes a clear understanding of what to do, where to go, and how to communicate with others during different emergencies.

Plan essentials:

Download the FEMA app to access resources, weather alerts, and safety tips. www.fema.gov and www.ready.gov are just a couple of good sites to check out.

Clarity and focus: In times of crisis, panic can set in. Having a plan provides a structured approach, helping you stay focused on necessary actions.

Communication: A plan should include communication strategies such as contact numbers, meeting points, and ways to stay in touch with family or emergency services.

Resource Management: A plan helps you prioritize resources like food, water, and medical supplies. Knowing what to do and when to do it can prevent waste.

Evacuation: For scenarios that require evacuation, a well-designed plan includes escape routes and meeting places. This can be crucial for ensuring the safety of yourself and your loved ones.

Community Coordination: In larger emergencies, community coordination is vital. Having a plan that aligns with local emergency services and community efforts enhances overall response effectiveness.

While having a plan is crucial, it is also essential to adapt it to different situations and regularly review and practice it. Your preparedness efforts should have basic emergency supplies like water, non-perishable food, a first aid kit, and essential documents.

Being prepared for emergencies involves having a set of essentials that can help you and your loved ones navigate various situations. While the specific items might vary depending on the type of emergency, here is a list of ten things you should have and why:

Water:

Why: Clean drinking water is a necessity. Dehydration can happen fast, and access to safe water is crucial during emergencies when regular water supplies may be compromised.

Non-perishable food:

Why: Having non-perishable food items such as canned goods, granola bars, and dried fruits ensures that you have sustenance even if regular food sources are disrupted.

First Aid Kit:

Why: A well-equipped first aid kit can help you address minor injuries. It should include antiseptic wipes, pain relievers, bandages, and any necessary prescription medications.

Flashlight and Batteries:

Why: Power outages are common during emergencies. A flashlight provides illumination, helping you navigate in the dark, locate supplies, and signal for help.

Multi-tool or Swiss Army Knife, gas shut-off tool, water shut-off tool:

Why: A versatile tool can be invaluable for various tasks, from opening cans to making makeshift repairs. It's a valuable item to have in your emergency kit. Many homes use gas for heat and cooking, so you should know where your home's shut-off valve is in case of a gas leak. Same for the water. Make sure you know where the shut-off valve is and how to use it.

Personal Hygiene Items:

Why: Basic hygiene items such as toothbrushes, toothpaste, soap, and sanitary supplies contribute to overall well-being during stressful times. They help maintain health and prevent the spread of illness.

Emergency Blanket:

Why: Lightweight and compact, emergency blankets provide warmth in cold conditions. They are essential for maintaining body temperature during emergencies.

Important Documents:

Why: Keep copies of essential documents, such as identification, insurance policies, medical records, and contact information. Store them in a waterproof container to ensure access to critical information.

Cash:

Why: During emergencies, having some cash on hand can help you purchase essentials or access services that may require immediate payment when electronic payment systems may be unavailable.

Communication Devices:

Why: A charged cellphone, a battery-powered radio, or a hand-crank emergency radio can help you stay informed and receive updates from authorities. Ensure you have backup power sources like portable chargers or extra batteries.

Remember to consider the specific needs of family members, including infants, elderly individuals, or individuals with special medical requirements.

Being prepared for emergencies involves a combination of planning, communication, and having essential supplies.

Create an Emergency Plan:

Develop a family emergency plan that includes meeting points, escape routes, and communication strategies.

Identify safe locations in your home for various emergencies. Each will be different depending on the crisis (Tornado, earthquake, flood, etc.).

Ensure that all family members are familiar with the plan and practice it regularly, especially if you have children.

Make sure each person has a go bag specifically tailored to them and a complete contact name, address, and phone number list.

Tip: If you live in a flood area, maybe laminate that list.

Stay Informed:

Monitor local news and weather updates to stay informed about potential threats.

Sign up for emergency alerts and notifications from local authorities.

Know Your Surroundings:

Be aware of the emergency resources available in your community, such as shelters, medical facilities, and emergency services.

Identify potential hazards in your area, such as flood zones or earthquake-prone regions.

Communication Plan:

Establish a communication plan with family members and friends. Designate an out-of-town contact person with whom everyone can check-in.

Ensure everyone has a list of important contacts, including emergency services.

Learn Basic First Aid:

Take a basic first aid and CPR course. Knowing how to provide immediate medical help can be crucial in emergencies.

Practice Evacuation Drills:

Regularly practice evacuation drills with your family. This helps ensure everyone knows what to do in case of an emergency.

Secure Your Home:

Identify and secure heavy furniture and appliances that could pose a risk during earthquakes or other disasters.

Install smoke detectors and carbon monoxide detectors.

Know where and how to shut off the power, water, and gas. Does it need a tool? Get that tool and keep it in an easily accessible place.

Prepare for Specific Needs:

Consider the specific needs of family members, such as infants, elderly individuals, or individuals with medical conditions. Ensure you have the necessary supplies and equipment for them.

Maintain and Update:

Regularly check and update your emergency kit. Replace expired items, update documents, and ensure that equipment is in good working condition.

Community Involvement:

Participate in community emergency preparedness programs. Being connected to your community can provide additional support during emergencies.

Remember that being prepared is an ongoing process. Regularly review and update your plans and supplies, taking into account any changes in your family, location, or potential risks in your area.

Know the emergency policies of schools and adult care centers if you have a loved one attending or in one.

Contact these places and find out what their protocols, procedures, and emergency plans are. Ask which emergency shelters are part of their plan, what emergency contact numbers/email/text they use, and how they plan to reunite you with your loved ones in an emergency.

Emergency Kit:

Prepare an emergency kit that includes essential items like non-perishable food, water, a flashlight, batteries, a first aid kit, medications, and essential documents. Keep this kit in an easily accessible place.

Consider having a portable phone charger in your emergency kit.

Emergency Contacts:

Maintain a list of emergency contacts and list important contact information, including emergency services (police, fire, medical), local authorities, utility providers, and other relevant organizations. Include both primary and alternative contacts, including family members and friends. Keep a hard copy and store this information on your phone.

Fire Safety:

Familiarize yourself with the fire escape routes in your building. Know where the fire extinguishers are located.

Have a smoke detector and carbon monoxide detector installed in your home/apartment, and test them regularly.

Security Measures:

Ensure that all doors and windows are secure. Consider reinforcing entry points with additional locks if allowed by your lease agreement.

Get to know your neighbors. A sense of community can be beneficial for mutual support and help when needed.

Renters/Homeowners Insurance:

Consider getting renter's insurance to protect your belongings in case of theft, fire, or other disasters. Make sure you understand the coverage and keep an inventory of your belongings.

Know Your Environment:

Be aware of the layout of your apartment complex and the locations of essential facilities such as stairwells, exits, fire extinguishers, and emergency services.

Know the policies of your apartment complex regarding emergency procedures.

Weather Preparedness:

Stay informed about the weather and any conditions in your area. Know the evacuation routes and the location of emergency shelters. Consider having weather-appropriate clothing and supplies in case of severe weather events.

Health and Safety:

Stay updated on local health guidelines and be prepared with necessary health supplies, especially during health crises or pandemics.

Maintain all hygiene practices to prevent the spread of illnesses.

Communication:

Establish a reliable means of communication, especially in the event of power outages. Consider having a battery-powered radio for updates.

Regular Safety Checks

Regularly inspect your apartment for potential hazards, such as faulty wiring or appliances. Report any issues to your landlord immediately.

Plan and Rehearse:

Develop an emergency plan for various scenarios, including fires, earthquakes, or severe weather. Practice evacuation drills regularly.

Remember that preparation is an ongoing process, and it's important to review and update your plans and supplies periodically. Always adhere to any specific rules or guidelines provided by your apartment management.

Chapter Three

Water

The average person needs 1 gallon of water per day, but you can get by with three-quarters of a gallon in a short-term emergency. With this amount of water, you obviously will not be using it to bathe or wash dishes; it is only for drinking or cooking. I would suggest buying water by the case if you are in an apartment with just one or two people. For storage, you might think about raising the height of your bed enough that a case of water can slide underneath or placing the case of water in the corner of a closet. Make sure that you use and rotate that water every year.

Tip: Make sure you rotate all your supplies regularly, check expiration dates, and buy items you can rotate into your normal daily life.

Now, I have a family of five. Keeping that much water on hand can be challenging unless you have the space. That would be 75 gallons of water for 15 days. I keep about that much on hand, but not all in cases of bottled water. I usually keep 6 to 8 cases of water from Costco in the garage, which I rotate into the house, and I replace them constantly. As for the rest, I have one large 55-gallon water barrel with a spigot that sits on a dolly with wheels to make it easy to move around, and the rest in 5-gallon stackable water containers. If you look online, you can find excellent stackable 5/10-gallon water containers or water barrels. I would not get larger containers unless you KNOW you will not have to move them around. It is a good idea to cover the top of your water barrel/container with an old clean towel or rag to help keep the dust off the top, and I have wrapped the spigot with saran wrap and a rubber band to keep dust out of it. The barrel and water containers sit nicely in the corner of the garage, out of the way. Again, I want to remind you to rotate your water at least once a year, use it to water your garden or whatever you need. Just make sure you change that water out regularly. As I write this, I am also being reminded, by the cat on my lap trying to help me type, to add a few gallons of water for your animals. Water weighs about 8 pounds per gallon, so plan for that, too.

Tip: Those 5-gallon cans/jugs of water/gas can weigh 40+ pounds each, so if you have an issue with that weight or someone in your home does, buy smaller cans/jugs.

I want to emphasize something. Never drink melted snow water, rainwater, or any water that is not from a public source or private well without filtering and boiling it thoroughly. In an emergency, if your home is on public water, also try to find out if that water supply has been compromised. Always boil your water. It is recommended that you boil clear water (filter the debris out of the water first.) for three minutes, to be safe, at a rolling boil (not just bubbling but a full rolling boil). However, I would boil it for five minutes, just to be safe. Then let it cool. After it is cool, put it in a clean, sterilized container with a tight lid.

Here's the alternative to boiling water: you can use bleach if you must. First, make sure that the water is free of debris by either letting the water settle so that all the debris drops to the bottom or by pre-filtering it with something to help remove the debris (Clean shirt, towel, coffee filter, etc.). Once the water is debris-free, add the water to a clean, sterilized container, and then add the bleach. For 1 quart (1 U.S. quart is equal to ¼ gallon, 2 pints, 4 cups, or 32 ounces) of water, add/use four drops of bleach, then let the bleach-treated water sit for 30 minutes. If done properly, there will be a very faint scent of bleach to the water. If there is not, repeat the process. Do not use scented or thickened (splash-less) bleach; only use regular bleach that is suitable for sanitation and disinfection, as stated on its label.

Tip: I will take a used 2-liter (2 L) bottle, clean it thoroughly, and then I will fill it with filtered water to about three-quarters full (remember water expands when it freezes), put the lid on tightly, then as the room in my freezer opens up, I put those 2 L bottles in the freezer because when the power goes out those bottles will help keep that freezer cold a bit longer, and as it melts that water is drinkable. As an added bonus, you can throw the frozen bottles in a cooler without all the mess of melted ice. Now, if you want, you can go out and purchase a countertop water filter system from Berkeley or Life Straw, which are both great at filtering water, but those are expensive, and not everyone can afford them. I keep a couple of the smaller Life Straw filters in my vehicle's emergency kit (which I will be going over later in the book) because I like to go out into the wilderness, camp, explore, and I have had vehicles break down.

Tip: To sterilize a dish, you need to thoroughly wash it in hot soapy water and then rinse it completely. Now get your unscented bleach that states it is for sanitation and disinfection (do not use scented or splash-less bleach), add it to a separate dishpan or sink. Many bleach bottles show the ratio and formula on the bottle, but here are the basics: 2 tablespoons of bleach to 3 gallons of water, or 1 ½ tablespoons to 2 gallons of water, and 2 teaspoons for 1 gallon of water. Fill your container with cool water, add the appropriate amount of bleach, then set the dishes in the water for two minutes. Once the dishes have been immersed for the appropriate amount of time, remove them and place them onto a drying rack without additional rinsing. Let the dishes dry completely; do not towel dry. It is crucial that you do the steps separately to safely sanitize your dishes.

Tip: Do not eat or melt yellow or discolored snow for drinking. Yes, sounds silly, but there are some....

That covers the basics for drinking water, but to add a supplement to this, I will tell you one of my wife's biggest fears is not being able to flush the toilet, so here are some ideas for that.

Tip: Always have a couple of weeks' worth of toilet paper on hand. My wife tells me that this is NOT an option, so there is that...

There are a few options; none of them are permanent, just short-term in an emergency-type situation. You can go out and buy a 5-gallon bucket and small garbage bags that fit; along with that, you can purchase a toilet seat that snaps onto the top of that 5-gallon bucket, which is excellent for short-term emergencies. What is also great is that you can use that bucket to store nonfood-related emergency items. If you must use the bucket in an emergency, definitely use garbage bags or poop bags to line the bucket, and when the emergency is over, I would suggest bleaching out the bucket inside and out, letting it dry before you store any items back into it. Now, if you live in a rainy or snowy area, you can use rainwater or melted snow to flush the toilet but do not drink that water without preparing it properly first. I also keep a few 5-gallon water containers full of tap water in our garage, and if I know a storm is coming, sometimes I will fill used milk jugs with water just for flushing toilets. As for keeping clean, I would suggest buying a case of baby wipes, hand sanitizer, and disinfectant wipes. They are not perfect for keeping clean, but they are better than nothing. Being clean and keeping clean is exceedingly important in an emergency, to avoid any food/water/human-borne sicknesses.

Tip: It takes about a gallon of water poured directly into a toilet bowl to make it flush. (Melted snow or untreated rainwater is perfect for this.)

Some of this can be adapted to apartment living. Depending on the size of the apartment, you will have to decide how much you can store. But almost everything I am suggesting can be pared down for 1 to 2 people and still fit into a smaller apartment.

Chapter Four

Food

If you take a minute and think about this, it is both difficult and easy to think of a food that you like, but also food that will keep without being refrigerated or that may need cooking. There are few foods that do not require cooking or water, so don't feel bad if you can't think of any. That's why you're reading this guide, to give you some ideas.

Food is a very personal choice and can vary in infinite ways, so this section will be relatively short, but I am sure exceedingly helpful. I must emphasize: Do not buy any food for emergencies that you/your family have not tried. The last thing you want is food that people do not want to eat.

Two weeks' worth of food in your home is not a lot, but there are little things you can add to make life a little more comfortable and to make sure that you don't have to leave your home until the emergency is over.

I won't go into the amount of calories a person needs per day to survive. You should be able to keep track of what you/your family eat over a two-week period. Take that list and subtract out any perishable items. Let us assume you do not have a generator to keep your refrigerator or freezer going, which means anything in your refrigerator and freezer will go bad in just a matter of hours or days (use that food first and fast), sometimes hours, depending on the temperature. A case of non-condensed soup is very easy to find, easy to store, and will keep for a few years, again check your expiration dates. But soup requires cooking. You might not have that ability (I will share some ideas on that later in the chapter). Now think about what you would eat that you do not have to cook. Bread will go bad in a few days, but in the meantime, you can use it for sandwiches. Yes, I know that sounds silly, but some people don't think of it. Peanut butter is an excellent source of protein if you are not allergic to it, and keeps well without being refrigerated unless verbiage on the container instructs you to keep it refrigerated, as in some organic types. Remember, this is a short-term emergency, so you're not going to get everything you want. Here are some suggestions:

Peanut butter/nut butter (non-refrigerated brand).

Ritz/saltine/fish/any crackers: These keep for a long period of time and can be used with peanut butter or other types of non-refrigerated spreads.

Granola bars/protein bars: These come in many flavors and types. Some are quite good, will last for a decent amount of time, and can be easily rotated into lunches or just snacks to keep them fresh.

Ramen noodles/cup of soup are great and easy to make but they require heated water.

If you like jerky, keep that on hand too.

Hard candies, if you have a sweet tooth.

Dried fruits keep for a decent amount of time and, in my opinion, taste great.

Nuts are another great source and even a small meal replacement. You can mix up the dried fruit and nuts when you're ready to use it and make a decent little trail-mix type meal.

Yes, you can go out and buy military-style MREs (Meals Ready to Eat). These last about five years, come in many varieties, and taste like rejected high school cafeteria food (If you've spent time in the military, you will understand. If you haven't, you're in for a nasty surprise! OK, just kidding.). Some of the MREs aren't too bad; try the crackers... but they are expensive for a family. However, for one person, for a couple of weeks, it's a simple solution.

There are also some great freeze-dried products out there that you can pick up from most grocery stores/camping stores/or online. Again these require heated water, so remember to keep track of the amount of water that you may need for the two weeks, and a way to heat it.

Canned (non-condensed, which means you do not have to add water.) goods are your best bet for short-term emergencies, but don't go out and buy a quantity of anything without trying it first. The last thing you want is to have to eat something that you dislike. You'll do it; you just won't like it. That goes for everyone else in your family. Make sure that you find things everyone will eat. We keep a couple of cases of non-condensed soup on hand and a case of chili, along with a variety of canned vegetables and fruits. Remember, this is only for a couple of weeks, not for the zombie apocalypse. Bonus: Zombies don't like canned fruits and vegetables.

Keeping dry goods for baking/cooking on hand is an excellent way to always have something, but there's a catch: You have to know how to cook things. You might be surprised at what you can make with a camp stove, Dutch oven, cast iron pan, and dry goods.

Get yourself a good-sized insulated cooler, which you will use for everyday products like milk, eggs, cheese, spreads, etc. Even if you have a generator that you are cycling to keep your refrigerator cold, it is a good idea to not open your refrigerator unless you have to, so keep the things you use most in a cooler. This is where you will put those 2 L bottles that you have frozen in your freezer, which will keep items cool. If you have four or more 2 L bottles, rotate them out as they melt down, no more than halfway, then throw them back in your freezer and refreeze when you cycle your freezer with your generator. If it is cold enough outside, you can also keep your cooler on your porch, but it is safer to keep it in your garage. Animals will smell that food and try to get into the cooler.

Tip: Make sure you have two weeks' worth of food and water for your pets or farm animals too!

And NO, for those that think an emergency is: I don't want to cook, or I forgot to go shopping. Ordering Grubhub or any food delivery is NOT a reliable source of food in an emergency... You know who you are.

Chapter Five

Cooking and Heating

A home with a fireplace/woodstove is great, but make sure you keep the stove and chimney well-maintained and checked annually to be sure everything is working properly. Some inserts cannot be used without power. Make sure you know what your fireplace/woodstove can do and if it needs power to operate.

There are many choices for safe indoor emergency cooking. Do a little online research and find something that fits your space and needs. Just be sure that what you choose is indoor-safe, and follow all of the operating directions.

I would also recommend that you get a battery-powered carbon monoxide detector. Many homes already have them, but to be on the safe side, go pick one up and install it properly.

I have found that dual-fuel type emergency cooking/camp cooking stoves work best for me. Some fuels like butane do not work well when it is cold.

Never ever use a camp stove that is not indoor-safe, indoors. If you can't find or afford one that is indoor safe, then get one that works outdoors and only use it outdoors per its directions.

When doing a word search for "indoor-safe," you will find that some products will pop up even if they are not indoor-safe. Make sure that you read the product description and its approved uses carefully. Also, consider what type of fuel the product uses. Is that fuel easy to get, safe to store, and doesn't use up a lot of space?

As with anything that has an open flame, make sure the cooking area around you and the product is well-ventilated and in a secure/nonflammable/stable area. If I have to use mine, I use it on a baking sheet on top of my home stove. Another idea is to have on hand a certified fire extinguisher, which you should have for any safety situation. Here are the meanings they will find on the side of a fire extinguisher; many will cover several classes of fire, and those are the ones that I would recommend keeping at least one in your kitchen and garage and a place that is easy to get to.

Not all fire extinguishers are the same. Review the verbiage on the side of the extinguisher. There are different fire classifications, and many of the extinguishers will cover several classes of fire. I recommend buying a multi-class extinguisher and keeping at least one in your kitchen and one in your garage in a place easy to get to.Of course, it's best to just not set things on fire... If you use the smoke alarm as a cooking timer, it may be a better idea for you to use/eat foods that do not require any cooking....

Here are the classes of fire extinguishers and what the classes mean:

A Class A fire extinguisher is for ordinary combustibles such as wood, cloth, rubber, paper, and any plastics.

A Class B fire extinguisher is for flammable/combustible liquids such as petroleum, grease, tar, oil, solvents, etc.

A Class C fire extinguisher is for fires that involve powered/energized electrical equipment.

A Class D fire extinguisher is for metals such as magnesium, zirconium, titanium, lithium, sodium, or potassium.

A Class K fire extinguisher is for fires in cooking appliances involving vegetable and animal fat or oils.

As for heating, I use a Mr. Heater Buddy. It uses small propane canisters and will last about three hours on high or about twice that on low. I have found that it will easily heat a small room to a comfortable, if not toasty, level in cold weather. So far, it has been easy to use and safe, but I make sure that I follow its instructions; I also go a little beyond and set it on some bricks while I'm using it. Again, remember to follow the product instructions and get yourself a carbon monoxide detector. It's best to be safe.

You can also buy an adapter that will fit a standard 5-gallon propane tank onto the heater. Just make sure your connections are solid, the propane lines are safe and not worn, that they are properly connected, and are away from direct heat or flame. The amount of propane you will go through depends on the amount of heat you want and how cold it is outside. On that note, I will add that the emergency cooking stove that I have also used propane and is indoor-safe, but I still use it only as needed, never for heating, and in a well-ventilated area.

Tip: A trick I learned years ago was this: Place three or four tea candles on a plate, then take a 6-inch terra-cotta pot and set it inverted (upside down) over the candles and plate, and then add a 10-inch terra-cotta pot inverted over the top of the 6-inch pot, like a Russian nesting doll set, one inside the other. The heat from this setup will last for a couple of hours and create a small area heat source, acting like a radiant heater. Just remember to keep it in a safe and nonflammable area. The holes in the bottom of these terra-cotta pots, inverted like this, will allow enough air for the candles to burn. I've used this tip several times in my life. Tea candles are relatively cheap. You can pick up 100 for about $12-$15 or less if you look for them on sale.

Another thing to add to your supplies is a quality cold-weather sleeping bag. Look for something that is rated for at least 20°F or less if you live in an extremely cold winter climate. Again, this is relatively inexpensive if you take the time to find one on sale.

Chapter Six

Power

Whole House Generators: If you can afford to buy one that can run the house and have a switch installed, that's wonderful, but many of us cannot afford that or are in a rental home. Getting a small-quality portable generator is a great alternative.

Only use generators or other gasoline-powered machinery outdoors, and keep them at least 20 feet away from windows, doors, and attached garages. Ensure generators and fuel are always used outside, and install operational carbon monoxide detectors on every floor of your home. Carbon monoxide, which is a colorless and odorless gas, can be fatal to you, your family, and your pets.

Protect the generator from rain or flooding. Keep it dry. Do not touch a wet generator or connected devices, as doing so may cause electrical shock. When connecting the generator to appliances, use heavy-duty extension cords. Allow the generator to cool before refueling, to prevent ignition from fuel spilled on hot engine parts. Carefully follow the manufacturer's instructions for safe operation.

Make sure that you get a generator that will run your essential appliances and that you calculate the wattage that your appliances will need. You can find that information on the door of a refrigerator or the back of many appliances. Our refrigerator is labeled at 6.5 amps. Assuming you are plugging the appliance into a standard 120-volt wall outlet, you will then need to multiply the 6.5 amps x 120 volts to get the average running watts, which in this case equals 780 watts. However, refrigerators and freezers also require an extra surge in power every time the compressor starts, which is often 2-3 times the average running watts. This means that the minimum size generator required for this appliance will be 1,560 peak watts. A kWh equals the amount of energy you would use by keeping a 1,000-watt appliance running for one hour.

For instance, If you use a 100-watt bulb, it would take 10 hours to use one kilowatt-hour. A 2,000-watt appliance would only take about half an hour. It all comes down to dividing the number of watts in an appliance into 1,000. A kilowatt (kW) is 1,000 watts and is a measure of how much power something needs to run. In metric, 1,000 = kilo, which means 1,000 watts equals a kilowatt. A kilowatt hour (kWh) is a measure of the amount of energy the appliance uses over time. In 2021, the average annual electricity consumption for a U.S. residential home customer was 10,632-kilowatt hours (kWh), an average of 886 kWh per month.

Think of it this way: A kilowatt (kW) is the amount of power something needs just to turn it on. A kilowatt hour (kWh) is the amount of power the device will use over the course of an hour. The average domestic refrigerator uses 350 to 780 W. That means the smaller portable 2000 W generators would work, but only for the refrigerator and not much else, except a coffee pot or to recharge batteries, maybe. So, you'd have to let your refrigerator cycle a few times to get cold; then if you had a freezer, you would have to unplug your refrigerator and then run your freezer for a few cycles to keep it frozen and go back and forth. That's a lot of work. I have three separate generators; two of them are 2000W, which means I can plug them together and get 4000W if needed. They are small and easy to carry and will run for 3 to 6 hours, depending on the power load. Then, I have a large 6500 W generator that is noisy but will power my freezers and my refrigerator, along with several other minor items I may want to charge or use. However, that generator is on wheels, is difficult to move around, is loud, and uses a lot of fuel. It's great to have available if I want to power everything at once. Most of the time, I use just one 2000W generator, which powers my refrigerator and my separate freezer. But again, make sure you calculate the peak wattage of the appliance and the generator.

If you have a generator, make sure that you take care of it and follow its maintenance schedule along with following all the manufacturer's instructions on how to use it. Generators should only be used outside, never in an enclosed space, and make sure you have 4 to 6 feet of empty space in all directions around your generator, depending on its size.

Tip: If you are looking to buy one, consider these things: Cost, quality, trusted name brand, power output versus your power needs, fuel tank size, fuel type, and ease of fuel storage. Also, think about the decibel (dB) range (how loud it is). The lower the number, the quieter it is. Consider its useability. Does it have a low oil shut-off? What is its weight? How big is it? Is it too heavy for you to move, or does it have wheels? If you think you'll need to parallel (connect two generators together to double the power) it to another generator in the future, does the generator come with that option? How do you start the generator? Electric start is great until the small battery dies, so make sure you can start it easily using the pull starter. Finally, do you have space to store it?

Let's talk fuel types. Portable generators generally come in three fuel types, and there are advantages and disadvantages to each type. Two to three 5-gallon gas cans (10-15 gallons) should get you through two weeks if used only as needed, and depending on the temperatures outside and what you're using your generator to do. Just remember that gas can go bad over time, so you'll want to rotate it into your car or lawnmower. Either way, make sure you use it and replace it a couple of times a year.

Gasoline is easy to get, but storing it in large amounts can be dangerous. If there's a widespread power outage, you'll have trouble getting the fuel since fuel pumps/gas stations require electricity to operate. Gasoline engines aren't as clean burning as diesel and may require more frequent servicing. Gas can start to go bad in about 6-7 months, but that can be extended with certain fuel-saver additives such as Sta-bil fuel saver, but do your research before using products like this.

Propane is the cleanest burning fuel; it never goes bad, but it is the least efficient fuel. Propane generators will need more frequent servicing than gasoline-powered generators but are much quieter. Propane fuel is easier to store in large tanks, which means less refilling.

Diesel is the most fuel-efficient and is less flammable than gasoline or propane. Diesel generators generally run longer without maintenance than gasoline-powered generators, and diesel generators are often louder than gas or propane models. Diesel can start to go bad in about 6-7 months, depending on temperature, how well it's sealed, and several other factors.

Thoroughly research any fuel you keep for safety, storage, and shelf-life before you store it.

Some generators you'll find are dual-powered (gasoline and propane) or even tri-powered (propane, natural gas, and gasoline). That is kind of cool, but I haven't tried one of these, so I don't know what kind of maintenance they require or how easy it is to switch between the fuels. Generators that run on regular fuel can be refueled at any time, so you can get more power right when you need it without having to worry about the weather conditions or the time of day.

The other type of generator is the solar-powered generator. Solar power generators are a great way for someone in an apartment to charge or power small appliances, but they're very expensive, and you may not have a place where you can put the solar panels so you can recharge the generator. But these generators are extremely quiet, require very little maintenance, and are safe to use indoors, unlike any other generator. Solar generators can only be recharged when the sun is out. Additionally, it takes time for the solar panels to charge the battery. A 100-watt solar panel would take over 9 hours to charge most mid-sized solar generator batteries. But I would highly recommend that someone living in an apartment building have one of these since it may be impossible for them to have an area where they can safely run a gas-powered generator. Just make sure that you get one large enough for your needs and have a place where you can open your solar panels. Most retailers will have a power calculator on their site. Some companies will sell the generator without solar panels or connections. Make sure that you have everything you need to operate, power, recharge, and fully understand and have read the instructions for the generator.

Tip: I have a long chain that I wrap through the generator handle and around a post and then padlock it. Years ago, I had a generator stolen during a power outage; the generator went off, and I assumed it needed fuel, but it took a few minutes to get out to check. Once I did, I found it was gone. Someone had literally just walked up and took it. I hadn't thought about the noise that it made and the fact that the noise just announced that I had power. Since that time, I have used a chain to secure the generator.

Tip: When buying a fuel-powered generator, try to get one that has a low-oil shut-off. These will shut down automatically when they get low on oil so they do not damage themselves. Also, pick up a quart or two of the oil required for the generator. You will not need much, but you will need it. Something else you can add to it is two funnels, one small one that will fit into the oil outlet of the generator and one wide one for pouring gas. Those simple items make it much easier to do these things.

Tip: Gas and Diesel can go bad over time and can ruin your generator. Once you are done with your generator for the season/emergency, let it either run out all the fuel or empty the fuel tank and then let it run until it dies.

Chapter Seven

First Aid

Tip: Make sure when buying a pre-made first aid kit that it either includes the following or add the items not included from the list below.

An emergency first aid kit should include the following items:

A book/booklet on first aid.

N95 masks

Adhesive bandages of various sizes

Sterile gauze pads of various sizes

Adhesive tape

Elastic bandages, various types/sizes, general, knuckle, butter-fly, dot, etc.

Antiseptic wipes or solution

Hydrogen peroxide

Rubbing alcohol

Tweezers

Scissors

Thermometer

Disposable gloves

CPR mask

Instant cold compress

Safety pins

Splint

Petroleum jelly

A couple of needles

Pain relievers such as acetaminophen or ibuprofen

Antihistamines for allergic reactions

Decongestants for nasal congestion

Anti-diarrheal medication

Antacids for heartburn or indigestion

Cortisone cream for itching and rashes

Hydrocortisone cream for minor skin irritations

Aloe Vera gel for burns and sunburns

Calamine lotion for skin irritations and bug bites

Prescription medications (if necessary)

I also include tampons and pads along with a small container of sanitizing or baby wipes.

Menstrual pads also make an excellent sterile and absorbent pad for topping wounds in an emergency.

A couple of lighters...for FIRE and stuff...

It is important to periodically check the kit for expired items and replace them as needed, include personal items such as allergy medication, epinephrine auto-injectors, and medical alert bracelets.

This sounds like a lot, but you most likely have many of these items in your medicine cabinet already.

Chapter Eight

Emergency Go Bag

When purchasing a backpack for a go bag, try it on, see how it fits, and make sure it's of a quality that will last. You don't need one so large that you cannot carry it, and you don't want one that chafes. I personally use a military-style bag with several pockets. Most of us will not be carrying the bag further than the car, but if you have to wear it, make sure that you do not overload it. Here's a list of some things that I keep in my bag. I will also say that each person in my house has an emergency go bag, and each bag is tailored to each person. The kids have things I do not, and vice versa; same for my wife. I will follow up with a direct list of what I carry and what my kids have. I suggest you build your kit or buy a kit and modify it for your needs and for your location.

First food: I keep 2 blocks of Datrex 3600 calorie food packs; remember these are 3600 calories for the whole packet, so follow the instructions. Consume a small amount at a time as needed. Each pack has 18 200-calorie bars, and a sealed pack will last up to five years. Make sure you check the expiration date when you buy it. Some questionable retailers will sell you a packet that is not expired but is very close. Two of those packets can keep me fed, maybe a little hungry, but fed for 3 to 5 days, depending on my rationing. I also have a few granola bars in there.

Make sure you taste what you have for emergency food. It would suck if you hated what you have!

I also keep a small packet of hard candies. It does not weigh much and can add a little comfort.

I keep a life straw that is small and filters up to a thousand gallons, or 4000 liters, and filters down to 0.2 microns, said to remove bacteria, parasites, and microplastics. Take a minute and read the instructions if you get it. In case of an extreme situation, I have a bottle of Potable Aqua tablets. I usually keep two or three bottles of water in the bag, also.

A minor emergency medical kit. My kit has all the basics: Band-Aids of various sizes, some Neosporin, a small bottle of Tylenol, Advil, aspirin, two types of tweezers (the pointy end ones and the regular ones), nail clippers, a small bottle of Betadine, a small package of Q-tips, a couple of sets of earplugs, a small bottle of Vaseline. I also include matches, a lighter, some needles, thread, super glue, a tube of Benadryl, 20 or so alcohol wipes, some hand sanitizer, a small tube of toothpaste, a toothbrush, a small bar of soap, small bottle of shampoo, a razor, small pair of scissors, and a small bottle of peroxide. Remember that this is only supposed to be for an absolute emergency. I have more items than these, but I feel that these are the absolute essentials for a small med kit.

I keep both an LED flashlight\two sets of batteries and a solar-powered flashlight in the back along with a small emergency hand crank radio with headphones, and a portable battery that will recharge my phone 5 to 6 times. I also keep a map of the county and state and a compass.

Clothing: Three pairs of socks, three pairs of underwear, two shirts (one heavy, one light), a lightweight rain-proof jacket, a sturdy pair of jeans, a good pair of gloves, an emergency poncho, an emergency blanket, a knit cap, a pair of swim trunks and a sweat suit/pants and shirt.

Basic Go Bag:

Food: Either freeze-dried camping food or emergency food bars, enough for 3 to 5 days. I would suggest buying a small amount and trying it before you put it in your pack. Remember that freeze-dried food will take up a bit more space. Remember to pack camp silverware and cooking kit if you're using freeze-dried food. It doesn't hurt to have a small cooking kit, even if you only have emergency bars in your bag.

Water: Three or four bottles of water; any more than that, and it will get heavy. Also, a water filter, something that will filter water down to 0.2 microns.

A small medical kit, buy a basic kit, and add any small items you feel you might need. I would suggest a pair of tweezers, a small pair of scissors, a wound disinfectant, some bug spray, a couple of small needles, a lighter, hand sanitizer (most sanitizer is flammable and can also help get a fire going), small bottle of Vaseline (can be used to protect small wounds, and if you have to hike can be used on your feet to protect from chafing, or as a simple lip balm, and a small amount on your tinder can help get a fire going). If you use medications, make sure you have 5 to 10 days' worth of them, but make sure to change them out frequently. My son is Type 1 diabetic, so I must keep his insulin in the refrigerator; I have both a small soft-sided cooler lunchbox and a small hard-sided cooler box (which the soft cooler fits into for extra insulation) and ice packs ready to go at all times. This also means I have an extra blood sugar tester and strips, needles, five sets of pump supplies, glucose tablets, and a glucagon pen in his bag. Some of those supplies spread out through the other bags. For my wife and daughters, I also add a small pack of tampons or pads and sanitary wipes; each pack has a roll of toilet paper and 3 to 5 1-gallon Ziploc-type bags.

Clothes: Socks, underwear, sturdy pants, pair of shorts, a lightweight rain-proof coat, a pair of gloves, a knit cap, two or three shirts, and at least one of them heavy. The type of clothing depends on where you live. Think about it, but remember to keep your choices balanced for both hot and cold.

My kids' bags all have most of the above, except the medical kit, which is very basic, with mostly just bandages and wound/scratch ointments. But I have also added pencils w/ sharpener, pens, notebooks, and a couple of small toys in each, which I let them choose. I also change out those toys and water and double-check the pack every year. It only takes a few minutes for each pack, and I have the kids involved with what goes in their pack.

In my go bag is also a small waterproof sealed bag that contains copies of my driver's license, my credit cards, my health insurance card, passport, copies of my kid's birth certificate, names and phone numbers of emergency contacts, doctors, friends, and family. Remember, in an emergency, don't try to call someone; in fact, switch your phone onto the emergency level to save battery life. If you must reach out to someone, text them if at all possible, because during emergencies phone lines are usually down or overloaded. A text is more likely to get through. Use your phone as an emergency tool.

The following is a list of things that I have and that you can use for your own bag. Modify the list as you need, of course, but make sure to have the basics of food, water, blanket, medication, med kit, and maps of your local area; yes, I said maps as in paper or plastic! Use those instead of your phone to save precious battery life. You may not get the chance to recharge your phone or your phone's backup battery.

Datrex 3600 calorie food 2 packs (Good for 5 years, read the expiration date).

Lifestraw or a filter like it. There are many great products out there.

3-4 bottles of water (I change these out annually).

Clothing for 3-5 days rolled tightly, which includes three pairs of socks, two light shirts and one heavy shirt, swim trunks, three pairs of underwear, one pair of sweats, and one good-quality pair of jeans. (Size-check annually, not that we ever gain or lose weight...)

Emergency blankets for each person. Not a full-size blanket but an emergency blanket, which you can pick up in the camping section of most retailers.

Emergency poncho for each person.

Quality light rain-proof coat.

550 cord/rope.

A small medical kit which includes: Bandages of various sizes, tweezers, small pair of scissors, small bottle of peroxide, small bottle of Tylenol, Advil, aspirin, Neosporin, alcohol wipes, Vaseline, bug spray, alcohol wipes, latex gloves, a small suture kit, needles, small tube of Benadryl, a small bottle of Imodium, potable Aqua pills, and medical tape.

Special medications and equipment for my son's Type 1 Diabetes needs.

LED flashlight with two sets of batteries.

Needle and thread.

Solar-powered flashlight.

Small emergency hand-crank radio.

At least 10,000mAh, the larger the better, backup external battery (check charge twice a year).

2 lighters/2 books of matches.

A small bag of hard candies.

A regular pen and a black Sharpie.

A notepad.

Sturdy gloves.

A Swiss Army knife.

A quality fixed-handle knife.

Small tool kit, with a Leatherman multi-tool/small pack of zip ties.

A small cooking kit that has a pot/pan/bowl, salt, pepper, and a spork.

A spool of strong fishing line.

8 to 10 fishing hooks of various sizes.

Map of the state.

A deck of cards.

A book.

A few Ziploc-type bags.

Toilet paper.

A toiletry kit, small toothpaste, toothbrush, soap, shampoo, razor, camp towel.

If you have a pet, make sure you have a small bag with the pet's basic needs ready. Keep it beside your own go bag.

Photocopies (front and back) of my driver's license, credit cards, health insurance card, passport, birth certificate, Social Security card, emergency/family/doctors contact information. I also have pictures of all these things on my phone. But if the phone dies, they are no good, so I keep photocopies too.

A small 2-man tent attached to the outside of the pack which I put it up and sprayed it with water-proofing when I purchased it. Plus, we keep the sleeping bags in a closet near the front door.

Remember, this is only an emergency bag. You could make it as heavy as could be and make it ready for the apocalypse. However, if you do end up needing it, it will be for a local weather-related emergency such as an earthquake, flooding, fire, snow, hurricane, tornado, etc., where any evacuation is most likely for a short period. And again, you will most likely grab the bag, throw it in your car and leave.

Chapter Nine

Vehicle

Having your car prepared for an emergency is just as important as having your home-and-go bag ready.

Again, I will say that this is not about preparing for the apocalypse! It's just being ready for any foreseeable circumstances.

Regular maintenance on your vehicle should be your number one priority for preparedness.

The question of what to add to a vehicle for emergencies is a lot like the go bag: It depends on your location, the type of weather in the area you live, the size and type of your vehicle, and above all, what you feel you may need in an emergency. Another thing to think about is that during seasons that may cause an emergency, such as earthquakes, tornados, snow, flooding, or hurricanes, I would recommend that you keep your gas tank as full as possible during those times of year.

In my two primary vehicles, I have basically the same items, but with a few more things in my four-wheel-drive Crew Cab. I live in the Pacific Northwest, and I have a family of five, so I have to consider that while preparing my vehicles. You do not need a four-wheel-drive crew cab if you live in downtown Los Angeles. It doesn't mean you can't own one, but good luck parking it.

My truck has so much junk in it, hidden underneath the seats and in toolboxes in the back, that we raided it for props on an independent film I worked on, actually on several films. But I will not list absolutely every piece of junk I have in there, just most of it.

I have everything that is in my go bag copied into my vehicles with the exception of a sleeping bag, tent, and medications and the addition of five more Datrex 3600 calorie food packs. Store food in a quality sealed container, or you may draw rodents into your vehicle. On top of that list, I also carry the following items:

A hammer.

A hatchet.

Jumper cables and emergency roadside kit.

Duct tape.

Electrical tape.

Two wool blankets.

A portable shovel.

A small 10 x 10 tarp.

A power converter.

Three more life straws.

Each door has two cupholders. In each of those, I have placed a bottle of water, plus 4 more bottles in my toolbox in the back. Additionally, just inside the garage is a 5-gallon water container that could easily be placed into the back of a vehicle, along with gas cans.

A couple of rolls of toilet paper and sanitary wipes.

A small box of pads and tampons.

A bottle of Tylenol and Advil, along with a full med kit.

Sunscreen.

Bug spray.

550 cord/rope

Zip ties

Three different flashlights, with a pack of batteries for each. One of the flashlights is rechargeable via a USB port in my truck.

An emergency rechargeable battery for my cell phone/laptop, charged/checked every 6 months.

Tip: Use the daylight-savings-time change to remind yourself to check your supplies and to change your smoke/carbon monoxide detector batteries in your home.

My toolbox is full of miscellaneous tools, screwdrivers, pliers, steel wool, wrenches, rubber fuel line, zip ties, hose clamps, emergency flat fix, rope, WD-40, a funnel, tire chains, and a couple of pairs of gloves.

A week's worth of medical supplies for my son's diabetic needs. (Not the meds; those are kept in the refrigerator and will be put into a small cooler that plugs into the truck.)

Several small notepads with pens and pencils.

Two books to read that I change regularly.

I wear glasses, and so do a couple of my kids, so I keep our old pairs in the toolbox.

Several different maps of the county, state, and country.

I have room and a garage, so I also have two emergency boxes right inside the door of the garage, ready to be put in the back of a vehicle, that contain emergency freeze-dried food, water, cooking utensils, basic clothing, and other miscellaneous items. There is enough there for at least two weeks. You may not have a garage or space like I do, but I would still recommend that you keep a 5-gallon water container someplace easy to get to and always full. And it would not hurt to have at least a small empty gas can to carry in the back of your car (yes empty, you do not want to keep a full can of gas in an enclosed vehicle). Having one in case you need it is, in my opinion, very important. It would not hurt or take up much room to have a midsized tote box somewhere easy to get to and ready to go. If you do not have to leave and there is an emergency, you'll still have the emergency items with you at home, but if you have to leave, you can easily grab that tote and throw it in your vehicle. Great places to store these items are underneath beds and entryway closets; even just having one large kitchen cupboard dedicated to only emergency foods is better than nothing.

In my home, I keep the normal filing cabinets, but I also have a fireproof lockbox that contains all of my very important papers. It's about 14" x 20", which is small enough to carry to the vehicle but large enough to hold all of the essential documents. I also do a computer system backup onto a portable hard drive every week, and that portable hard drive goes back into the lockbox.

Chapter Ten

Beyond the Basics

Since the chemical train derailment in Ohio, if you live near a chemical plant or train rails, you may want to go further. Add a Tyvek suit and respirator for each person in the house.

If you are worried about a radioactive, chemical, or biological incident, Get a roll of 6mil plastic, enough to cover each window, vent, and door. If you don't want people seeing light from your home at night, maybe consider using black plastic.

Duct tape.

Box of N95 masks.

A battery-operated or hand-cranked radio and extra batteries to stay informed about emergency instructions.

Copies of important documents such as identification, insurance policies, and medical records, driver's licenses, passport, and credit cards, front and back. A copy is better than nothing.

Also, keep your super important papers in a fireproof safe. Include the above, plus add car titles, birth certificates, passports, immigration documents, insurance policies, bank account passwords, and account numbers, along with a list of your most important passwords for your email, bank accounts, etc.

A flashlight and extra batteries.

A map of BOTH your local area AND one for your state. Yes, I said map: That big paper thing that no normal person can refold. Your phone may not work. Best not to count on it.

Have a secondary and even third place to meet family if you have to evacuate and are separated.

Have a pet carrier, harness, and leash handy. Only for the animals, not the kids or wandering husband...well, the leash maybe....

Tip: If you have a cat, even if they never used a harness or leash, it is a great thing to add to your kit. Put the harness on the cat before you put them in the carrier. Some cats will bolt as soon as the carrier is open, but if you have the leash and harness on them properly and are ready for it, they will not be able to run off. The same goes for your dogs. Remember, animals can sense danger/panic/fear and may not act "normally." Best to be safe and not lose a pet.

If you can afford it, have your pet microchipped in case the pet gets lost in an emergency... NO, you cannot microchip your kids or husband...

Keep a copy of addresses and phone numbers, again with the paper thing, in all your vehicles.

Choose an out-of-state friend or relative to reach out to in case you have to relay messages. Make sure everyone in your family has the person's address, phone, and email information.

Cell phones may not work if you're trying to call out. A text message has a better chance of getting through, even if it takes longer to successfully send, or if you have to resend it a few times to get it to work. In a crisis, many phone lines and companies get overwhelmed, so try texting first. If you have a WI-FI connection or internet connection, try email too.

Establish a regular schedule for communication updates, especially during prolonged emergencies. This helps keep everyone informed and minimizes confusion.

Tip: During the large fires in the last few years, I have learned that a big box fan and a large, good-quality furnace filter put together will help filter out the air in your home. Use tape or bungee cord to attach the filter to the outside of the box fan, and poof! A cheap instant air filter.

Chapter Eleven

Quality

When it comes to being prepared, one of the most important things you can do is invest in quality items. This is especially true for emergency and survival gear. In the event of an emergency, you want to be able to rely on your equipment and supplies without worrying about them failing or breaking.

Here are a few tips for investing in quality items for your preparedness kit:

1. Do your research: Before making any purchase, take the time to research different brands and options for the item you are looking to buy. Read reviews and compare prices to make sure you are getting the best value for your money.

2. Look for durable materials: When purchasing items such as tents, backpacks, or sleeping bags, look for materials that are known for their durability and weather resistance. This will ensure that your gear lasts longer and holds up well in tough conditions.

3. Consider multipurpose items: When possible, invest in items that can serve multiple purposes. For example, a good multi-tool can be used for a variety of tasks and saves space in your kit compared to carrying individual tools.

4. Check warranties: Some companies offer warranties on their products, which can give you peace of mind knowing that if something were to happen to the item within a certain time frame, it could be replaced or repaired.

5. Learn how to use and maintain your gear: It's important not only to invest in quality items but also to know how to

properly use and maintain them. This will ensure that they last longer and perform at their best when needed.

6. Don't forget about food and water storage: When storing food and water for emergencies, make sure you are using high-quality containers that are specifically designed for long-term storage. Improper storage can lead to spoilage or contamination, which defeats the purpose of having these supplies on hand.

Remember that investing in quality doesn't necessarily mean spending a lot of money. There are many affordable options out there that are still reliable and durable.

The CDC, FEMA.gov, and ready.gov have basic lists for everyone. There are a few things on my lists that are not included in theirs but, in my opinion, are important, simple additions that could make things a little easier in an emergency.

Chapter Twelve

Lists and whatnot

In the event of an emergency, having a well-stocked emergency kit and being prepared with important documents and information can make all the difference. Below are some lists to help you get started on building your own emergency kit and staying informed during a crisis.

Things to know:

Where is the water main shut-off, and do you have the tool to shut it off?

Does your home have a furnace, stove, water heater, or other appliance fueled by gas? You need to know where your gas shut-off value is and have the tool to shut it off. You also must know how to light and relight your pilot flame if your appliance uses one. Look up your specific appliance online and print out the instruction/user manual. Keep that printout where you can refer to it in an emergency.

Where is the safest place in your home to be in an emergency? Each home and emergency will be different. Check out Fema.gov and BeReady.gov for specific information on this topic.

Use Daylight savings time changes to remind you to check your supplies/smoke/carbon monoxide/ batteries, and recharge any portable/rechargeable power packs you have.

List 1: Emergency Kit Must-haves

- Water (one gallon per person per day).

- Lighter.

- Notepad and pen.

- Change of clothes.

- Non-perishable food items (canned goods, energy bars, etc.) and a can opener.

- First aid supplies, including medications (pain relievers, bandages, etc.).

- Flashlight and extra batteries.

- Multi-tool or Swiss Army knife.

- Personal hygiene items (toilet paper, hand sanitizer, etc.).

- Emergency blanket.

- Copies of important documents (ID, insurance, medical records).

- Cash in small denominations.

- Small battery-operated radio, with batteries. OR a multi-powered emergency radio.

- Communication plan and who/when/how to contact and relay messages in an emergency.

List 2: Documents to Keep in a Fireproof Lock Box
- Birth certificates.

- Social Security cards.

- Passports or other forms of ID.

- Insurance policies (homeowners/renters, health, life).

- Medical records and prescription information.

- Property deeds and titles.

- Will and estate planning documents.

List 3: Important Phone Numbers to Have on Hand

It's always important to have easy access to important phone numbers in case of an emergency. Here are a few numbers to keep handy:

- Local police department/fire department.

- Poison control center.

- Doctor's office.

- Pharmacy.

-Major utility companies (electricity/gas/water).

-Emergency contacts for family members/friends.

-School/work contacts.

List 4: Evacuation Checklist

If you need to evacuate your home during an emergency, here are some things to consider bringing with you:

-Medications/medical supplies.

-A change of clothes and comfortable shoes.

-Toiletries/personal hygiene items.

-Water and non-perishable snacks.

-Cash or credit cards.

Some cool gadgets to get if you can afford them:

USB-Rechargeable camp lights: I have both a lantern and puck lights that recharge via USB, and they are great!

External Battery Packs 10000mAh or larger power bank. I have 6 in various sizes, 10000mAh to 50000mAh. I use them on set, traveling, and when the power goes out. My kids also have a smaller version that they carry in their backpacks for school. Make sure to charge them every 6 months.

USB LED Lights- These can plug right into a battery bank and will last a long time, depending on the output of your battery bank.

Bluetooth speaker. When the power goes out, we like to listen to Audiobooks as a family. Psst... My book Solar Reboot is an Audiobook... Hint hint.

Rechargeable hand warmer, these things are great!

NOAA Weather Alert Radio solar/crank radio with a built-in rechargeable battery, that can be recharged by solar/hand crank/power plug, or USB cord, or regular batteries. The more power options, the better.

An indoor safe heater like the Mr. Heater Buddy; I love mine. Just BE SAFE and FOLLOW the directions on how to use it.

If you are in an apartment, take a look at the many portable solar power stations. The prices are dropping, and these are safe and QUIET for an apartment. Even if you cannot recharge them via solar, you can still make sure they are charged, via plug-in, and waiting for a power outage. Some are powerful enough to run a small refrigerator for a short period of time.

There are portable refrigerators that can plug into your car, too. I have one for my son's insulin.

The most important thing is to be calm, take time to evaluate the situation, and to be prepared. You cannot prepare for everything, but you can be ready for most things. My philosophy is "Better to have it and not need it than to need it and not have it."

Finally, don't spend money you don't have. Watch for sales, and get the absolute necessities first. Try out whatever you buy and know how to use it.

ABOVE ALL, be safe, be calm, and think.

Also By

"Solar Reboot"

a multi-award-winning thrilling apocalyptic adventure.

And my debut book of poetry.

"Life Therein: a moment at a time."

About the Author

Matthew D. Hunt

Matthew D. Hunt lives in the Pacific Northwest, is a proud father of three, an award-winning author, and an Emmy-nominated filmmaker known for his innovative storytelling and captivating visuals.

Throughout his career, Hunt has worked on a variety of T.V. series, short films, documentaries, and feature films. He has also written the multi-award-winning novel "Solar Reboot" which has been widely praised for its engaging characters, innovative world-building, and thought-provoking exploration of the human condition in a post-apocalyptic future. Hunt's debut book of poetry, "Life Therein: A Moment at a Time," is a stunning poetry collection that takes readers on a journey from the depths of despair to the heights of joy; the book captures the essence of what it means to be human. Through evocative and powerful poems, the author explores themes of love, loss, life, and humor.

In addition to his creative work, Hunt is also a dedicated teacher and mentor, having taught and lectured on writing and film at several conventions around the United States, including the honor of being a judge and lecturer for the Ms. Wheelchair USA competition. His passion for storytelling and commitment to excellence continue to inspire others in the creative community.

Find Matthew's work on Amazon,

IMDb, or mdhuntbooks.com

Notes space:

Phone Numbers:

Check lists: